Johs. B. Thue

The Flåm
Railway

Towards the west

A person from western Norway is drawn towards the west, towards the fjord, the sea and the ocean. From Myrdal station down the Flåmsdalen valley the forces of the instinct fill up our senses. We eat the nature, we smell the ocean. The ocean lies in the valley, cooled by soft winds. Rain and sun, sun and rain. Alder copses, juniper, sallow, and polled birch trees. A profusion of wildflowers – garlic mustard, early purple orchis, and sea Mouse-ear. Shrubby willows hang on tenaciously along the small brooks. Fields and hillsides covered by a green lustre. Rocks polished by wind and avalanche released by the water from the ocean, in clouds and mists.

The silent mountains and the scree-grey rocks give us this feeling that time is standing still, as if it has stood still since the creation of time. And then, all of a sudden, a shriek from pitch-black ravens rising from a dead animal. An echo rolling in between the mountains, heavy and unreal. We may sense the presence of eagles, deer and martens around us, and in the tropical light the poisonous foxglove blossoms.

Down in the valley we feel that the hay is spiced, as nowhere else in this world. Like the first man on his way towards the ocean, across the mountains, we hear the ringing and gurgling sound from the summer fjord licking the salty slopes of naked rock.

Nobody travels the Flåmsdalen valley. It is rather an encounter with smells, mountains, and visions. A journey within ourselves where the instinct creates all the images for our inner eye.

Southern Norway and the Flåmsdalen Valley

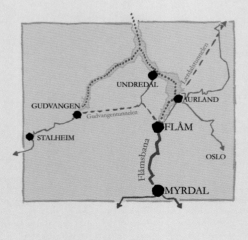

VEG   TUNNEL   JERNBANE   FERGE

Contents

1

The Flåm Railway
– A National Treasure

The fjord pony among the railway lines

Every year close to 600 000 passengers travel on the Flåm railway line. This is actually one of the biggest and most popular tourist attractions in the country. The high number of passengers, which is indeed sensational, has not come of its own accord. There must be many reasons why so many people come to Flåm to travel the 20-km-long railway line along the Flåmsdalen valley up to Myrdal station, 856.6 metres above sea level.

The locomotive El 9 at Flåm station.

The carriage interior.

The Flåm Railway is a mountain railway line. The impressive and beautiful countryside, and the efforts of international tour operators have turned this railway line into one of our major tourist attractions. At the same time, there's something special about this line. It is like a living organism, it has defied politicians, it has survived the threat of being closed down, and has gone its own ways. It lives like an obstinate fjord pony, and negotiates the terrain like a

fjord pony, the very symbol of power and ability to survive. It meanders easily and quietly up from Fretheim, then starts climbing up the screes and steep mountainsides, all the way up to the mountain plateau with its pack-load. And like the fjord pony, it gets its nourishment from its own valley, powered by the electricity generated at the Kjosfossen waterfall.

The fertile Flåmsdalen valley.

The steepest railway line with standard gauge

There are about 140 railway lines in western Europe, and these have been evaluated in terms of adventure. 19 of the mountain lines are awarded three stars which is the top mark. Two of these three-star lines are to be found in Norway, the Bergen Railway and the Flåm Railway. According to the reference book Gebirgsbanen Europas, "Die Flåm-bahn ist ohne Zweifel eine der imponierendsten Gebirgsbanen der Welt" – without any doubt the Flåm Railway is one of the most impressive mountain lines in the world.

Why is this railway line described in such a favourable way? Part of the answer lies in its technical aspects. The Flåm Railway is the steepest line in northern Europe with standard gauge (1435 mm). The gradient is 55‰. It is indeed a unique construction we find up towards the mountains in the inner regions of the Sognefjord. The Flåm Railway was designed and built using very steep gradients, on narrow

The Flåm train passes along and through extremely steep mountainsides, here shown cutting through the crags at Høga.

The train at Pinnali, before disappearing into the moutain once more.

ledges in the mountainside, and with tunnel loops through a typical western Norway countryside. One can hardly imagine that nearly 80% of the 20-km-long line has a gradient of 55 ‰ and that the smallest curve radius is only 130 metres. Is it any wonder that railway enthusiasts are thrilled about this railway line?

The laying of tracks started from Myrdal in the summer

seminars, studies, and cultural events in the capital. We travelled by train up the valleys in the summer night. At the break of dawn on a sunny June morning we stood on the platform at Myrdal station. Fridtjof Nansen, our first athlete and national hero had also stood at this place in the mountains when he had lost his way on a late winter evening in 1884:

"I was looking down a precipice of several hundred feet and saw the dark abyss of a narrow valley – the Flåmsdalen valley." He was standing on top of the cliff of Myrdalsberget.

These precipices and cliffs were later to be conquered by a masterpiece of Norwegian engineering and construction. Myrdal owes its existence to the railway. Everything was focussed on the railway.

When the Bergen Railway was under construction, a transport road was built up the valley from Flåm to Myrdal, the so-called "Rallar road" to get access to the line up in the mountains.

This road continued from Myrdal to Finse/Haugastøl. In the summer months after the Bergen Railway had been opened, there was much traffic between Flåm and Myrdal station by horse and cart (chaise). On the busiest days, there could be between 30 and 40 of these one-horse chaises in use at the same time. At the bottom of the steep rocky ascent called "Myrdalskleivene" with its 21 hairpin bends and a gradient of one in five, it was only allowed to let the horses pull one passenger at a time. The following sign was put up on the lower hairpin bend: "Be gentle against the horse and walk the hill up (sic)".

Myrdal station, with station master's residence, was built before the Bergen Railway was completed. The one-and-a-half-storey houses at Myrdal are all built of rock. The architect was P.A.Due, who also designed most of the buildings along the Bergen Railway line. In addition, there were built a shop, bakery, office, depots, engine shed, community hall, staff residences, and barracks in the area around Myrdal station. The line Voss – Myrdal was opened for temporary traffic in the period 1 July – 15 September, 1906, and from 16 June – 21 December, 1907. Since 10 June, 1908, the Bergen Railway has been open, first for construction purposes, and

in regular operation from 1 March, 1908. In 1950 there were 142 permanent residents at Myrdal, in 1960 the number had been reduced to 118, in 1970 there were 91, in 1980 40, in 1990 only 11 remained, and in 2001 the number of inhabitants was six.

In 1935, a new first floor was added to the station building. The ground floor was also rebuilt. Today's station build-

ing was completed on 1 June, 1994, after comprehensive reconstruction work. For Myrdal, then, the railway represented a revolution, an unequalled transformation.

In our minds we could draw the following conclusion: from the mid 19th century, the railway and the steamships became the symbols of the new Norway. The first railway construction took place practically without any planning

The old railway restaurant was a charming place with a special atmosphere and a stylish interior.

involved. The terminal stations were located where the
local initiative was strongest. "Therefore we got the best
railway network in the whole world", as a Norwegian historian puts it. Later on came the plans – the endless railway
plans. The Flåm Railway had always been a contentious
issue, between experts, between regions, and not at least
between politicians.

Steam locomotive ready for departure from Myrdal.

At some places there is only space enough for the train and the river.

"Take your seats – shut the doors, please!"

We are standing, then, at Myrdal station on the Bergen Railway line. On this sunny summer's day the station area is teeming with tourists. To the sound of the old cry "take your seats – shut the doors, please!" we get onboard the train. We are on our way, rolling on rails down to Flåm. As a guide we have a manuscript after the legendary conductor and narrator Einar Johnsen (1914 – 1991). He charmed all travellers with his accounts of this railway line that he loved so much and that meant so much to him. The first kilometres down the mountainside, the train glides in and out of snow shelter tunnels and through a couple of shorter tunnels down to Vatnahalsen. The countryside opens up to

All aboard!

Below: Snow comes early at Myrdal station.

The station area at Myrdal.

Vatnahalsen Hotel was situated like a fairytale castle, surrounded by mountains and lakes. The hotel was built in 1896 and was originally a sanatorium. It was destroyed by fire during World War II and was rebuilt in 1953–54 in a completely different style.

a view of a mountain plateau. In the far distance rises the
peak of Tarven with its eternal snow and ice, and in the
foreground is the lake of Reinungavatn like a glittering pearl
of green glacial melt water. After a sharp curve to the north,
the train makes a stop at Hylla (literally the shelf or ledge),
an opening in the mountainside immediately after the train
has entered the "Vendetunnelen" (the loop tunnel). At close
range we can witness man's eternal fight against the forces
of nature, the fight of the railway engineer, the fight of the
railway navvy! Several hundred metres straight down we
can discern the river like a silver ribbon along the valley,
and on the opposite side of the valley we see the precipitous
mountainside with the railway track cut out on a narrow
ledge. We get another breathtaking view once the train
emerges into the daylight again at Baklia. But, as the train
has made a full circular turn inside the mountain, the view

The Kjosfossen water-fall "hibernates" in wintertime.

Wild forces at play in the Kjosfossen water-fall. The ruins of the old water-power station to the right.

is now on the opposite side.

After this, the conductor announces over the loudspeaker that the next stop is Kjosfossen. At this point tourists may get out on the platform to enjoy the view of an impressive waterfall. Looking up towards the horizon we can see and hear the white, roaring cascades of water rushing towards us. It is a magnificent display when the river water is broken

down into foam on the sharp ledges in the mountainside below. Framing the main waterfall a number of smaller brooks plunge from the adjacent precipices. The whole mountainside is alive. Water gives life. Running water – as it has always been – is our greatest life-giving force.

In these two pictures you can see five levels of railway. Both pictures are taken from the same place. In the larger picture you can discern the steep rocky ascent called "Myrdalskleivene" with some of the 21 hairpin bends up to Myrdal.

"The post must be delivered"

Before the train enters the long tunnel called Nåli (literally the needle), we can follow the line down the mountainside from Myrdal. Within a distance of one kilometre, we can see five levels of railway track – four of these belong to the Flåm Railway, the fifth and uppermost is part of the Bergen Railway line. At the same time we can see how the old transport road winds itself up the steep Myrdalsberget. This road was built in 1895–96 to get supplies up to the Bergen Railway construction across the mountain plateau. The road was built for transport with horse and carriage. But now the horse is gone, and the old road across the mountains lies open for bikers and hikers. In the years leading up to the completion of the Flåm Railway, this road was virtually the only connection from the Bergen line down to the Sognefjord. The bulk of the mail to and fro the villages in Sogn was thus transported daily by horse and carriage – in winter sled – from Myrdal to Flåm and then onwards by local steamer – and vice versa. For more than a generation the postal transport was carried out in this way by the two

Horse and chaise, but also a favourite playground for trolls.

brothers Guttorm Fretheim and Ola Brekke in Flåm. It was often hard going for man and horse. Nevertheless, the mail was usually delivered on time.

The troll and the archetypical Norwegian

At the exit of the Nåli tunnel we can see the mountain farm of Kårdal down in the valley bottom. The old turf-roofed farm houses are nestled together by the river bank and the white-foaming waterfall. The landscape around this farm consists of green fields along the river. However, once we exit the next long tunnel at Blomheller, we become fully aware that the countryside in the Flåmsdalen valley is not only idyllic and picturesque. The many scars and traces in the mountainsides caused by avalanches and falling rocks bear witness to the fact that the forces of nature many a time have caused fear and panic among the wayfaring people. The best known – and the most feared – of these avalanches is the Trodlaskreda, which many times every winter wakes up the whole valley with thunderous bangs when the snow masses sweep the mountainsides clean on their way down to the valley bottom. The avalanche has something of the forces of the troll in it. In the mythological world, trolls lived in all the mountains, and they became a symbol of the archetypical Norwegian. From the train we can see across

Troll. By Theodor Kittelsen (1906).

The Flåmsdalen valley seen from Vatnahalsen.

to the other side of the valley with its 500–600-metre-high and nearly vertical gully or the track of the avalanche of Trodla. There is hardly any tree or bush left in the gully, and the rock surface has been swept clean and polished. The massive heaps of snow accumulated at the foot of the mountain, withstanding even the warmest summers, are a visible

testimony of the enormous masses of snow carried by this
avalanche. Trolls could not stand sunlight. If they saw
sunlight, they burst. But the snow masses at the foot of the
Trodlaskredet avalanche prove that not even the sun always
comes out a winner over the troll, the forces of darkness.

After crossing the valley and the river at Melhus, the

The El 11 at the Vidme level crossing.

tourist must once again move over to the opposite side of the railway carriage to see wild and untamed "mountainscape". Only the brooks plunge down the mountainside – with the white-foaming river far down in the dark and deep canyon. The sun and the light never reach this place. This is

The Rjoandefossen waterfall with its free vertical drop of 140 metres.

horizon becomes wider. The eye catches a picture of nearly everything that characterises the Norwegian landscape.

Colour photos of this landscape so full of contrasts have been used on the covers of brochures and travel guidebooks both in Norway and abroad. Along the river banks in the valley bottom lie the well-kept Flåm farms with their lush, green fields and orchards, and in the background the majestic Vibmesnosi rises to the sky, adorned by the silver band of the Rjoandefossen waterfall.

"The first song sung to me"

The church at Flåm dates all the way back to the Middle Ages. There was probably a stave church at the site of the present church. The church as we see it today, dates from about 1670. At first the church walls were tarred, but in the mid 19th century, the church was painted white. In the 1960s the white paint was washed off, and once again the church has been tarred. The church is richly decorated with

The Flåm church was erected in 1670. The church site itself is much older, and there was probably a stave church on this site in the Middle Ages.

paintings depicting deer, fox and lion on the walls. The altar cloth is a medieval knight's coat from Venice.

At the farm next to the church we can see a tall monumental stone, erected in memory of the Norwegian poet Per Sivle who was born on this farm. This is where he heard "his mother's song at the cradle" as he puts it in one of our most popular and beloved songs. Per Sivle was one of the country's leading writers towards the end of the 19th century. With his pen he took his readers back to the Middle Ages, to the golden age of Norway's power with its North Sea Empire. He loved Flåm, where his mother came from. "Dip your hand into the Sognefjord, take a good grip and give it my best regards", he once said rather emotionally to an acquaintance from Flåm he came across in Oslo. Per Sivle's life ended in tragedy.

All the good qualities in Per Sivle came from Flåm, according to himself.

Left:Today Flåm has a population of close to 400.

Flåm is one of the great tourist magnets in Norway. On this picture the Flåm Railway meets huge cruise liners. The new deep-water dock is an important precondition for this successful interaction between rail and ship. The big cruise liner docked here is S/S Norway.

After three kilometres from Flåm church, the train has said farewell to the Flåm valley. Our journey has come to an end. Flanked by 1000-metre-high mountains, the train rolls slowly into the terminal station of Flåm, and we get our first glimpse of the blue Aurlandsfjord, this southern branch of the main Sognefjord cutting in between the steep, jagged mountains. The lush vegetation of plants, bushes, and trees around the station area at Flåm is good enough evidence that we have entered a mild and fertile fjord climate.

Today less than 400 persons live in Flåm, and like

Fretheim Hotel in 2001.

Bustling life on the Flåm station area.

The centre of Flåm has undergone a major facelift in the last few years. Today Flåm can offer modern facilities for cruise liners.

many other similar villages, the population has been drastically reduced in recent years. Most people make a living of tourism and transport activities linked to tourism. In Flåmsdalen valley there are still a few farms with a full agricultural production.

In 1994 there was a significant change in the operational concept of the Flåm Railway. The municipality of Aurland, the Savings Bank of Aurland, and SIVA (The Industrial Development Corporation of Norway) joined forces to establish a new company called Flåm Development Ltd. This is the company that operates the Flåm Railway today. The rail network is owned by NSB (Norwegian State Railways). Rolling stock is leased from NSB, but also from other railway companies in Scandinavia.

"Huldra" – the wood nymph

If you are born under a lucky star, you may catch a glimpse of the wood nymph. She appears occasionally at Kjosfossen, in the same way as she can appear anywhere in the Norwegian countryside. According to the folklore tradition, the wood nymph was a spirit living underground, in hills and crags. The name is derived from the verb "hylja" which means to hide or keep secret. And it was in this hidden, secret world that the wood nymph and her spouse lived. "Hulder" is used as a generic term for "the little people" who lived like ordinary people with their fields and farms, houses and homes. The belief in the huldre people, "the little people" is no specific Norwegian phenomenon. The Finns have their saivo people, the Celts their sidh people.

Men felt a strong erotic desire for the wood nymph. Even as late as the 1930s, there are accounts of men who have had wild, erotic encounters with the wood nymph. The wood nymph was actually exceptionally beautiful, face to face, that is. From behind, it was a different affair altogether. She had a cow's tail, and sometimes her back was hollow. From time to time she married ordinary people.

In fact, the wood nymph is mostly associated with the Norwegian mountain farm tradition. She had big cows which were either blue or grey. It was possible to get hold of these animals if you threw a piece of steel over them. In this way you could also get silver and tablecloths. We have many stories of bridal silver which supposedly was taken from wood nymphs, and there are wood-nymph table cloths in Årdal.

In the mountain farm tradition, there are also accounts of farm girls who had been accosted by "the little men" who wanted to marry them. These girls were never left alone until they married properly.

Can you see the wood nymph by the waterfall at Kjosfossen?

Wood nymph drawn by Ridley Borchrevink (1898–1981).

"The little people" had many musical talents. Sometimes you could hear them singing and playing tunes. Many fiddlers learned tunes from them. People could listen to this music for hours.

Folklore experts disagree about the origin of the conception of the wood nymps. Some tend to think that the wood nymphs are meant to be regarded as the souls of the dead. Others are of the opinion that they are meant to be looked

upon as fictitious beings of a psychological and social nature. They may also be understood as natural fictions.

There is a similarity between the belief linked to dead people and that of the wood nymphs. People firmly believed that the soul kept on living after death. One belief was that the soul stayed where the body was, either in the grave, in the hill, or in the water if the person had drowned.

Willy Brandt's reflections in the Flåmsdalen valley

Before the ordinary railway operation was started in 1942, the road between Fretheim and Myrdal was much used by travellers. They came by boat to Flåm from villages further out in the Sognefjord. Then they were driven for a stretch up the valley or they slogged on foot all the 20 kilometres up to Myrdal, suitcase in hand.

Willy Brandt, the prominent German politician, was one of those who used this road. Brandt came to Norway as a political refugee in the early 1930s. By and by he established close links to the Norwegian labour movement. Through its political youth organisation – the AUF

– he was sent on a lecture tour to many places in the country. He was in Høyanger and Vadheim, the two industrial towns along the Sognefjord at that time. He may also have given a speech for the labour youth organisation in Flåm. This was one of the best and biggest labour organisations in the county of Sogn og Fjordane. The railway had radicalised a sleepy western-Norway village.

Willy Brandt walked the Flåmsdalen valley. He describes this walk in his book Links und frei (To Fight for Freedom). He describes the impressive countryside in the Flåmsdalen valley, but also the peace and quiet that he experienced in the farmyards and around the homes under the towering mountains. Willy Brandt writes that his reflections are primarily linked to the desire that everybody in the whole wide world could live such a good life. Here the people lived in peace, they lived in harmony with nature – and even conquered nature – at the cliffs of Myrdalsberget. But at the same time, the young political refugee reflects on the Norwegian fight for freedom, which was so different from all other freedom fights in Europe. The freedom fight was linked to the idea of democracy – an extended democracy. In Europe these ideas were implemented by people in the cities. The city air gives freedom, they said down south. In Norway things worked differently. Here there were people from the rural areas who carried through the big democratic changes. Thus, a journey up the Flåmsdalen valley may lead to reflections with views and perspectives. Similarly, our thoughts may still wander. "The birds may travel so far and wide" writes Per Sivle.

3

The history

A long-drawn political process

The history of railway development in western Norway is
long and slow. The railway line Bergen – Voss was completed in 1883, and in the 1890s there was a general consensus
that the so-called Lærdal line was the most favourable
gateway to the Sognefjord.

The intention was that this line should be extended to
Gudvangen and Voss. In other words, the railway line would
more or less follow the same line as the present trunk road

FRETHEIM HOTEL
FUNKSJONÆRBOLIG
VERKSTED OG REMISSE
STASJONSBYGN
HOVEDSPOR
FRETHEIM DAMPSKIBSBRYGGE
ST.

The suggested location of Flåm station according to plans from 1928.

Left: The quay at Fretheim just before World War II.

between Bergen and Oslo. There was no other alternative. However, the Norwegian parliament ("Stortinget") decided to extend the railway line from Voss to Taugevatn. The county council of Sogn og Fjordane put forward the idea of the Flåm Railway for the very first time in 1895. However, this idea was also opposed locally. The municipal council of Aurland wanted the line to go to Vangen. According to some, having a terminal station at Flåm would lead to problems because of the ice conditions on the fjord in wintertime. And the opposition to the Flåm Railway came from all quarters, from Aurland and Lærdal, but also from those who wanted the line from Voss either to Gudvangen or to Vik. Politicians vehemently maintained that the Flåm Railway would always be a "surrogate with a touch of railway smell". However, as in so many other similar cases, somebody has to cut through and put an end to the discussion. In this case it was Ingolf

Fretheim ran a grocery, steamship agency, telephone exchange, post office, hotel, and posting station.

Elster Christensen. He was born in 1872 and became county governor in Sogn og Fjordane in 1910. Later on he became a member of "Stortinget" and cabinet minister. In 1909, he put in the decisive word for the Flåm Railway with the following formulation: "The railway line that can provide the shortest and the least expensive line from the region of Sogn to eastern Norway, is the best one for Sogn. The railway line that can remove most of the Sogn products away from the Bergen market, is the best one for the regions of Sunnfjord and Nordfjord." In this way he convinced the whole county to rally round the Flåm Railway alternative. People from various regions of the county were not to compete with each other on the Bergen market. This competition cut prices. People from Sogn were to trade with Oslo, and the eastern market would become available by means of the Flåm Railway. Ingolf Elster Christensen's arguments were later echoed by others.

The destiny of the Flåm Railway was far from being decided in 1909. Now cars – automobiles – made their entry, and many suggestions were put forward to the effect that a car road would be a better alternative between Fretheim and Myrdal than a railway line. The chief administrator of Norwegian Public Roads came to the county council to present the road alternative, but he failed miserably in persuading the county politicians. The opposition to the Flåm Railway continued, however, which county governor Christensen summed up like this:

"The destruction of the Flåm Railway became a battle-cry for everybody who wanted to be called economists, even after the railway had been decided three times by "Stortinget", and after 5–6 million kroner had been invested in it. It has frequently been brought up for discussion – sometimes the attacks come from Bergen, at other times from Oslo, from the road authorities and the railway authorities, from the outside and from the inside."

Autumn colours at Flåm

Once more we return to our initial question: why does the Flåm Railway enjoy such a strong position among the Norwegian tourist attractions? Obviously, this has to do with the fantastic countryside. The Flåm valley enjoys a special position in the tourist trade. The 44-kilometre-long Flåm watercourse runs from the Omnsbreen glacier (1500 m a.s.l.) at the watershed to the Hallingdal valley until it reaches the sea at Fretheim which marks the head of the Aurlandsfjord. The upper section of the river is called Moldåa. Then it rushes through the Såtedalen valley along the Bergen Railway line down to the lake of Grøndalsvatn. The river is framed by snow glaciers, green pastures, and further down by birch forests. There it runs into the three lakes of Klevavatn, Seltuftvatn, and Reinungavatn like a string of pearls. From Reinungavatn the river plunges headlong into the 238-metre-high Kjosfossen, an impressive waterfall cas-

M/S Nesøy at the Fretheim quay.

Autumn colours at Flåm.

cading down on several ledges between dark crags into the wild canyon. Then it flows in a succession of waterfalls and rapids all the way down to the Flåm church. From this point onwards in its flow towards the sea, the river is more famous for its salmon and trout than for its waterfalls. Building the Flåm Railway took more than half a century from its conception until the first train rolled down the tracks from Myrdal to Flåm. As early as when the initial plans for the construction of the Bergen Railway were discussed, it was suggested an attempt be made to get a railway connection from this line down to the villages in the regions of Sogn and Hardanger. In the 1870s, the forest master Hans Gløersen,

also known as the "father of the Bergen Railway", put
forward the idea that it might be a viable solution to build
a railway line in the precipitous Flåm valley down to the
Aurlandsfjord. On 1 March 1894, the Norwegian Parliament
("Stortinget") decided to build the Bergen Railway, but no
decision was made in terms of constructing any branch
line down to the Sognefjord. It was not even on the agen-
da. Before the construction of the Bergen Railway, very
few people knew about this wild and beautiful Flåmsdalen
valley. The valley was remote and closed off with just a
narrow, winding and steep road fit only for pack-horses. But
then – in the years 1895–96 – like "a moment of truth", the

situation changed. It was decided to start building a transport road through the valley, from Fretheim up to the high mountain plateau between Myrdal, Hallingskeid and Finse. Agile horsemen with their horses and carriages were soon to become a familiar sight for the locals in the valley. And those who lived in the valley became directly or indirectly involved in the construction. And this construction was the Bergen Railway – the monumental, national building effort of the late 19th century, immediately prior to the termination of the union strife with Sweden.

Never officially opened

3o years earlier, people in Bergen had marched in a torchlight procession, wild with joy, to celebrate the Stortinget decision to build the Bergen Railway. However, the decision made in 1923 by the Stortinget to allocate money so people in Sogn could be connected by rail to the outside world, did not cause the same degree of festivities and jubilation. It was not in their nature to show their emotions openly. We know, however, that the station master Stenberg at Myrdal assembled the whole station staff when the cable came with the announcement that a railway line was to be built through the Flåm valley. In order to mark this happy occasion, he let everybody gather around the flag pole where the flag was hoisted and pictures were taken.

After the decision by Stortinget on the building of the Flåm Railway, the construction could get underway in the spring of 1923. The construction of the Hardanger Railway between Voss and Granvin was started a couple of years earlier. The construction manager there was senior engineer Peder Lahlum who had an office at Voss. He was then put in charge of the construction of the Flåm Railway as well, and this continued until 1935, when the Hardanger Railway was opened for traffic. The site managers for the Flåm Railway – with office in Flåm – were throughout this period the assistant senior engineers Johan Johnsen, A. Kielland, and Rolf Aksnes. Our newly elected king, Haakon VII, accompanied by many of his cabinet ministers were present at the triumphal arch of flags and garlands near Ustaoset in the autumn of 1909, when the railway tracks from the east and west were joined – to mark the opening of the Bergen Railway. There was no such solemn celebration when the first train between Myrdal and Flåm came puffing in at the station by the Aurlandsfjord. The country was at war, and this was not the right time for any celebration or festivities. The train came "puffing" because in the first years, the traction units were small steam locomotives. The railway line was fairly quickly opened for passenger traffic, and in the autumn of 1944, the first electrically operated trains were taken into use. In July, 1941, the Norwegian State Railways (NSB) decided that "the railway line Myrdal – Flåm was to be called the Flåm Railway".

The Flåm Railway
Documentation Centre

The Flåm railway museum is located in the old station building at Flåm. Since 1995 one has worked systematically to collect photos, written documentation and objects linked to the history of the Flåm railway and railway history in general.

The Flåm Railway Museum was opened in 1994 in the annex of Fretheim Hotel. The museum moved from one place to another until 1999 when a leasing agreement was signed with "NSB Eigedom" (NSR Property). Then parts of the station building at Flåm were taken into use for this purpose. The main reason for establishing the Flåm Railway Museum was a new massive interest in the Flåm Railway. In earlier times people showed little interest in collecting documentation on this railway line, and nobody undertook the task of preserving unique source material. Now people deemed it of vital importance to take care of objects and written sources related to the history of this railway line. The museum has now collected protocols and other documentation material which have been properly catalogued and stored. In addition,

key objects have been taken care of which may shed light on the development of the Flåm Railway. A case in point is the newly restored locomotive El 9, a switching tractor, an inspection truck, and some smaller rail tricycles. The Flåm Railway Museum also has a comprehensive photo collection. New pictures and written material are added to the collection all the time.

Behind the museum the newly restored El 9 locomotive is displayed.

The Flåm Railway Museum received annual funding from Flåm Utvikling AS. The work was to a large extent based on the idealism of the railway enthusiasts. In 2005 this privately owned limited company was taken over by Aurland Ressursutvikling AS.

4

The labourers

The "rallar" (the railway navvy)

The "rallar" is a special concept in the modernisation history of Norway. "He ate all things new out of the open air," as the well-known Norwegian proletarian writer and "rallar" Kristoffer Uppdal puts it. The typical "rallar" came from Sweden and migrated from one construction site to another. But the Swedes were gone when the work on the Flåm Railway was started. The Norwegian construction

workers had taken over. They were frequently referred to as "bus" or "slusk" (rowdies) in Norwegian. The typical rowdies still had a lot in common with the "rallar" in terms of appearance and behaviour. The broad-brimmed hat, the tobacco chewing, the red bandanna singled him out from other workers. The "rallar" and the "slusk" migrated from one construction site to the next. They had no fixed domicile and lived in barracks months after months, year after year. They went wherever there was work to be done, no matter where it was to be found. One would perhaps have thought that these navvies were individualists. Some of them were, undoubtedly, but at the same time they showed solidarity to each other and to the group they belonged to. They played a key role in the establishment of the Trade Union Congress in Norway, through their own trade union "Norsk Arbeidsmandsforbund" (the Norwegian Union of General Workers).

The story of Arne Stenersen may serve as an illustration. He settled down in Berekvam in the Flåmsdalen valley where he built a house and established a home. He came from Sigdal in the neighbouring county of Buskerud. His father had also been a navvy, first on the Dovre Railway, later on at the Rauma Railway. When Arne was seven, his family moved to Otta in order to be closer to the father's workplace. In 1924, the Rauma Railway was completed, and the Flåm Railway was the next major construction. The whole family then moved to Flåm, and Arne was just 15 when he earned his first wages on railway work. After Flåm, he worked first on the construction Kristiansand – Moi, then on to Helleland at the rebuilding of the line to Jæren. Finally he worked on the Nordland Railway.

Many of the navvies working at the construction site were later given permanent employment in the NSB (Norwegian State Railways). Sjur Gjerde from Flåm worked on the Flåm construction site from beginning to end, Magne Bjørnestad writes. When the trains started rolling, he was first employed as a line worker, then as a line-keeper. He kept this job until he retired.

The "rallar" road

From days of old there was a steep and hardly passable road from Fretheim up to Kårdal, the uppermost farm in the valley. This road was frequently made impassable because of avalanches. In order to establish a reliable supply line between the Sognefjord and the Bergen Railway, something had to be done. At the same time, the road had to be extended from Kårdal to Myrdal. The first step to be taken was to improve the road between Fretheim and Kårdal. From Kårdal up to Myrdal a four-kilometre-long construction road was built with 17 hairpin bends in the mountainside. The gradient was formidable – one in six, that is one metre increase in altitude for every six metres! From Myrdal the road was then extended through the Moldådalen valley, past the lakes of Reinungavatn and Seltuftvatn. It was at Låghelleren that the well-known Norwegian writer and essayist Nils Kjær coined the term "Vestlandsfanden" (literally the western-Norway devil). This character represented the counter-culture forces in the young nation of Norway. He was against all consumption of alcohol. "He detects the smell of alcohol in our glasses", Nils Kjær wrote. Besides, he was an ardent supporter of the new dialect-based Norwegian

The "rallar road" is today a much used road for bikers and hikers. Bicycles can be rented.

language. He always dressed in black. He "invaded" the
Norwegian Parliament ("Stortinget") with his laws and
regulations. "Vestlandsfanden" is still a concept in the
Norwegian cultural debate. Kjær was immensely impressed
by the Flåmsdalen valley. He wrote that "in a short while
this valley will become famous all over Europe. Photographs
of this valley will be sold at Boulevard des Italiens and at
Piccadilly. Competing valleys in Norway and abroad will be
justifiably forgotten, and will seem insignificant in compa-
rison with this newly discovered natural beauty spot". This
was written in the early 1900s and history has certainly
proved him right.

By horse and hand

The transport of equipment for the construction of road and rail demanded people – labourers. The old construction worker Sjur Gjerde told the local historian and writer Magne Bjørnestad that the safest way to get work was to buy a horse.

– I was lucky, says Sjur – My father had a horse, and thus I got my first job at the age of 15. The whole station area was filled up with masses of excavated rock. It was there I had my first job as a construction worker with horse and dumping wagon. The biggest job I had was at the Nåli tunnel which is the longest tunnel on the Flåm Railway line.

All transport in the tunnels was carried out with small trolleys with dumping wagons and sidetip, all moving on rail. The gradient of the rail line is fairly steep so the main part of the job was to brake the dumping wagons on their way out. Then they led the horses into the tunnels again. They tried to replace the horse with both petrol and diesel-run locomotives, but these locomotives polluted so much in the tunnel that horses were reintroduced. – It is fair to say that the horse was the most reliable means of transport, Sjur Gjerde ascertains. However, there was also use for the strong man lumbering forward like a bear. The story goes that Daniel Vidme from Flåm was a well-built and extremely strong person. He could walk up the steep road of Myrdalskleivene carrying a load of 60 kilos on his back. Once he carried a stove from the lake of Låghellervatn to Finse – a load for four persons!

Another giant of a worker was "Lærdalsborken" (literally the braggart from Lærdal). He had the reputation of carrying as much on his back as a horse could. He was even paid as a worker with horse. Stories of such extremely strong men are found at many construction sites.

Practically all the tunnels on the Flåm Railway have been excavated and made passable by manual drilling. All loading of rocks was done by hand using scrapers and boards. The only device they used to make the work less strenuous was the so-called stump-puller which was used to lift and move the biggest rocks. As for the excavation of the tunnels, it always started with drilling a hole in the centre of the intended tunnel opening about a metre from the ground with two-three holes on either side. The first holes were struck almost horizontally, slanting upwards. Drilling a hole of 2 metres' length was considered to be a good day's work. In the ceiling of the tunnel they drilled so-called "Englishmen" and these had to be drilled vertically. The bottom section of the tunnel was the last to be drilled. The construction workers called this "stop-

A work team during the construction of the Flåm Railway.

Changing rails in the old-fashioned way.

ing" the tunnel. Drilling holes in the bottom of the tunnel was often such heavy work that two men were needed for the job.

In the long tunnels the work teams could consist of nine men. Three workers loaded, three drilled, and three transported the excavated masses out of the tunnel. In the shorter tunnels six men usually made up a work team. The rate of progress was about two metres a week.

For the people of Aurland it was very common to work on railway construction sites. People of all age groups had been working on the Bergen Railway construction for many years, most of the young ones working with various types of supplementary work in the aftermath of the gigantic construction on the mountain plateau. Most of the construction workers who came to Flåm had been transferred from other sites when these were completed. Many workers came from the Rauma Railway in the Romsdalen valley.

Even in those days it must be admitted that working on these sites was not a very lucrative affair, to put it mildly. Most of the work was carried out on contract for less than two kroner per hour. For those who worked on a day-to-day basis the payment per hour was just above

1 krone. If you had a horse for transporting the masses out of the tunnels, it was easier to get work, but no compensation was given for the horse. The working methods were cumbersome and old-fashioned. It was only in the long

tunnels of Nåli and Vatnahalsen that machines were taken into use for drilling. All the other tunnels were excavated by manual drilling. Most all types of work operations were done manually and it is hard to imagine today how back-breaking and strenuous this work must have been.

Torstein Ølmheim

Torstein Ølmheim (born in 1939) from Flåm is a third-generation railway man. His grandfather came from Ølmheim in Sogndal and started as a railway worker on the Bergen Railway. He also worked for some time on the Flåm Railway. Torstein's father, Anders, was badly injured in an accident at his workplace. In the line of duty he was subjected to electric shock and lost one of his legs. After some time he was able to start working again with loading and unloading goods on the Flåm quay.

As soon as Torstein had finished his military service, he started as a candidate in the NSB (Norwegian State Railways). He shovelled coal on the steam locomotives on the Bergen Railway. Then he studied at the Railway Academy in Oslo in 1963. He then became "2nd man" on trains between Ål and Hønefoss on the Bergen Railway. For one year he was also stationed in Narvik to work on the rail transportation of iron ore.

In the mid 1960s he returned to Flåm, now as an engine driver. The old locomotive El 9 –at present displayed at the Flåm station (see picture on p. 61) – now became the tool of his trade.

When we are talking with Torstein, asking him how many passengers he has transported between Flåm and Myrdal, he answers with a smile on his face: – Honestly, I have no idea, but there must have been thousands. Remember that for long periods we had to run three sets because of the high number of passengers.

– Were you never frightened by the great responsibility you had on this steep railway line with canyons and crags everywhere you looked?

– No, I have never been scared. We drove slowly, which is necessary on the Flåm Railway. Down from Myrdal the speed never exceeded 30 km/h. Up from Flåm, however, we could make 40 km/h.

– Did you get good contact with the passengers?

– Oh, yes. The best part of the job was to talk with railwaymen from other countries. They always contacted me and were hungry for information about this special line. I can remember that there were even railway people who came all the way from New Zealand. They travelled on my train and we established good contact, he adds.

– And now you have retired?

– Yes, I stopped working at 62. I was not tired of my job, but I got really fed up by the administrative mess in the NSB organisation.

Torstein Ølmheim, then, belongs to a typical railway family. His brother, Edvard, is an engine driver on the Flåm Railway. He, too, got the chance "to come down again". This means that he was able to get back home to Flåm.

Edvard Ølmheim has also played an important role in the organisation called Friends of the Flåm Railway, which was established in 1987. This organisation had its roots in the local community of Flåm, and has done an incredibly important job to make the railway better known to the general public and thus used more.

The last service trip of Torstein Ølmheim in 2001.

The locomotives

EL 17

Manufacturer ....Henschel
Year(s) built 1981; 1987
Numbers built 12
Maximum speed ....150 km/h
Traction engine ....4 x NEBB BOg3855
Power ....4090 hp/3000 kW
Length above buffer ......16.3 metres
Weight ....64 tonnes
Axle arrangement ....Bo'Bo'
Flåm Railway 2227, 2228, 2230, 2231, 2232

SJ X10

Manufacturer .... ASEA
Year(s) built .... 1982 – 1993
Maximum speed .... 140 km/h
Power .... 1280 kW
Length above buffer .... 49.868 metres
Weight .... 100 tonnes
Axle arrangement............. Bo'Bo' + 2'2'

Flåm Railway locomotives leased from Sweden during summer seasons in the 1990s

EL 11

Manufacturer.................Per. Kure / Thune
Year(s) built....................1977 – 1984
Numbers built................17
Maximum speed.............70 km/h
Traction engine ....2 x ASEA SJ1103
Power..............................940 hp/690 kW
Length above buffer ....12.7 metres
Weight.............................61.3 tonnes
Starting tractive force ....157 kN
Axle arrangement...........Bo'Bo'
Flåm Railway 2110, 2092, 2098

EL 9

Manufacturer Per. Kure / Thune / NEBB
Year(s) built.....................1944
Numbers built................3
Maximum speed.............60 km/h
Traction engine ....4 x NEBB EDTM423
Power..............................968 hp / 712 kW
Length above buffer ....10.2 metres
Weight.............................48 tonnes
Starting tractive force ....108 kN
Axle arrangement...........Bo'Bo'

BM 64

Manufacturer.................Strømmen
Year(s) built....................1934
Numbers built................3
Maximum speed.............50 km/h
Traction engine ....4 x NEBB EDTM384
Power..............................632 hp / 464 kW
Length above buffer ....16.3 metres
Weight.............................38.1 tonnes
Seating capacity 38

NSB TYPE 25

Manufacturer.................... Hamar (19), Thune (3), Baldwin (9),
                                 NMI (6), and SLM (5)
Year(s) built....................... 1901, 1909, 1911–1914, 1917, 1919, 1922
Numbers built.................. 42
Forward / reverse speed ... 40/40 km/h
Length above buffer .... 8.670 metres
Weight varied between .... 33.2–36.2 tonnes dependent on type letter
Axle arrangement C

SKA 207.3

Manufacturer.................NEBB, Thune (750 mm gauge)
Year(s) built ....1932 (rebuilt to standard gauge
                                 in 1946 by NEBB/Skabo)
Numbers built................2
Maximum speed.............35 km/h
Engine ....2 x NEBB GGM022
Power..............................44 hp / 32 kW
Length above buffer ....5.1 metres
Weight.............................11.6 tonnes
Axle arrangement...........Bo

Technical information

Length of the railway line ....20.2 km
Height difference...........................863.2 m
Upper station – altitude................865.6 m
Lower station – altitude ....2 m
Maximum gradient ....55 ‰ or 1:18
Stretch > 28 ‰...............................16 km or 79.3 % of the line
Minimum curve radius ....130 m
Gauge...1435 mm
Voltage ....15 000 V – 16 2/3 Hz
Driving time...................................55 minutes
Brake systems.................................5
Tunnels 20
Bridges...1
Water tunnels.................................4
Halts...8

Number of passengers

1945	51.000	1998	350.606
1948	45.000	2000	374.738
1959	119.522	2001	398.948
1964	115.461	2002	414.770
1969	120.850	2003	417.540
1974	169.032	2004	459.144
1979	176.000	2005	475.033
1984	200.617	2006	536.693
1989	228.568	2007	582.286
1990	253.980	2008	544.190
1992	313.132	2009	516.180
1994	379.625	2010	547.000
1996	346.615		

Stations

Station	Altitude (m)	Myrdal (km)	Flåm (km)
Myrdal	866	0.00	20.20
Vatnahalsen	811	1.13	19.07
Reinunga	768	2.20	18.00
Kjosfoss	669	4.40	15.80
Kårdal	556	6.34	13.86
Blomheller	450	8.40	11.80
Berekvam	345	10.51	9.69
Dalsbotn	200	13.90	6.30
Håreina	48	17.21	2.99
Lunden	16	18.60	1.60
Flåm	2	20.20	0.00

Tunnels

Name	Length in metres	Years of construction	Manhour per metre	NOK/m	NOK/hour
Furuberget	424.00	1926 – 34	149.00	380.00	1.56
Spælemyren	24.60	1929 – 30	180.00	391.00	1.55
Dalsbotn, lower	206.60	1930 – 35	179.00	380.00	1.44
Dalsbotn, upper	154.30	1925 – 28	136.00	446.00	1.80
Høga	59.20	1927 – 28	161.00	467.00	1.83
Timberheller	172.60	1932 – 33	145.00	333.00	1.40
Geithus	139.20	1934 – 35	172.00	389.00	1.43
Sjølskott	39.20	1931 – 35	131.00	365.00	1.69
Reppa	132.90	1926 – 28	139.00	423.00	1.85
Melhus	177.5				
Melhusgjelet	11.10				
Blomheller	1029.60	1924 – 35	163.00	410.00	1.69
Nåli	1341.50	1924 – 35	140.00	386.00	1.68
Kjosfoss	478.40	1924 – 35	150.00	417.00	1.73
Bakli	195.10	1924 – 34	142.00	406.00	1.86
Tunnel p.1668	22.70				
Tunnel p. 1692	14.00				
Vatnahalsen	888.60	1924 – 34	116.00	384.00	1.99
Toppen, lower	79.90	1925 – 26	128.00	444.00	2.37
Toppen, upper	101.40	1926 – 29	146.00	420.00	2.09
Total	5692.40				

Brief historical overview

1871	The first plan put forward by the forest master at Voss, Hans Gløersen, as a part of the Bergen – Oslo – Stockholm railway line.
1893 – 1903	Assessment of various line alternatives: Myrdal – Fretheim or Voss – Stalheim – Gudvangen.
1904 – 1916	Assessment of various rail alternatives: rural tram, cable railway, rack-railway, adhesion rail, various gauges – standard gauge or narrow gauge (1067 mm), as well as assessment of various traction alternatives: steam, petrol – electric or electrically operated.
1908	The Norwegian Parliament ("Stortinget") decides on the Myrdal – Fretheim line in the National Railway Plan. The number of passengers estimated at 22 000 annually.
1916	"Stortinget" decides on the adhesion alternative and a standard gauge of 1435 mm.
1923	"Stortinget" decides on electrical operation and passes an allocation plan for the whole construction.
1924	A significant year for the project! The construction itself gets underway. 20 tunnels in all and 18 of these to be excavated by hand. Excavating one running metre of tunnel implied one man-month work. 5 692 metres of tunnel altogether and 20.2 kilometres of railway line were to be completed. The work force varied between 80 – 280 persons. The progress of the construction varied with the national economy, which in turn depended on international economic trends. Before the construction was completed in 1942, two workers died in accidents.
1936	The laying of tracks was started. The tractive force was provided by a small steam locomotive (NSB type 25a – No. 228).
1940	The completion was planned to coincide with the delivery of electric locomotives and the hydro-electric power station at Kjosfossen. Thus it was not until 1942 that one had aimed at opening the line. At the outbreak of war in April 1940, five kilometres of track-laying remained. The Germans demanded that the work on the line should be stepped up. As early as 1 August 1940 the line was opened for traffic. This, then, is the actual opening date of the line.
1940–42	Freight transport with steam locomotives (NSB type 25 – Nos. 228, 422, 424, and 425). Maximum eight axles with manual screw brakes on each carriage. The driving time down the valley was 65 minutes, 80 minutes in the opposite direction. Water tower at Berekvam.
1941	Passenger traffic allowed from 10 February after three locomotives installed extra counter-pressure brakes on the steam cylinders and the track brakes. The Ministry decides that the name of the line is to be Flåm Railway.

1942	The construction formally handed over to NSB – Bergen District.
1944	The electrification and the hydro-electric power station at Kjosfossen completed. The transformers for the electric locomotives (El 9) were sabotaged and blown to pieces by a Norwegian resistance group in Oslo. The electrical operation did not get started until 24 November with an electric motorised car from the Hardanger line (BM 64).
1947	Electric locomotives are delivered (El 9) and the first aluminium carriages taken into use. After 11 years, the steam locomotives are no longer used.
1940–42	Average annual increase of 11% in the number of passengers.
1953–1969	The number of passengers is stabilised at 115 000 per annum up until 1969. The Flåm Railway is rarely referred to in a positive way by the media. The general discussion and media reports mainly deal with the possible closing-down of the line. However, gradual improvements of the product are introduced, such as installing loudspeakers in the carriages, and constructing a platform at the Kjosfoss halt (1968).
1958	Direct sleeping-car to Oslo. This was a major political break-through.
1969–1979	The traffic increases by approximately 10% annually, and the number is kept stable at about 175 000.
1976	The railway station restaurant at Myrdal is closed after nearly 70 years.
1978	The morning express from Oslo now stops at Myrdal station.
1979–1989	Substantial increase in the traffic, especially in the early 1980s. The discussion concerning the closing-down of the line abates. The traffic figures remain fairly constant at about 200 000 travellers per year.
1982–83	The traction force is changed. After 35 years of faithful service the El 9 locomotives are being phased out. The rebuilt El 11 is taken into use with the motorised car unit BM 69 from 1984.
1993–1994	New station building at Flåm is opened in 1993, and the railway reastaurant at Myrdal station is reopened in 1994. The village of Flåm is connected to "the outside world" by a new road.
1989–1995	The traffic increases dramatically and climbs to 380 000 passengers a year. This figure makes it one of the country's major tourist attractions.
1998	The Flåm Railway is taken over by Flåm Development Ltd. The purpose is to ensure a year-round operation of the railway line.

Thanks to the Flåm Railway Museum and Visit Flåm for pictures and documentation.

Photo:
THE FLÅM RAILWAY MUSEUM 15, 16, 19, 22b, 28, 42a (Jon K. Nesse), 52 (Jan Kirby), 53, 54 (Jan Kirby), 55 (Jan Kirby), 62, 64, 69 (Jan Kirby), 70, 74a, 74b, 75a, 75b, 75c, L. NES 60, S. NES 23, 24a, 24b, 26, 27, 41a, 41b, 46, 48, 61 NORSK JERNBANEMUSEUM 62, HELGE SUNDE 6, 8a, 10, 11, 12, 18, 20, 22a, 30, 32, 35, 38, 40, 50, 58, 71, 74c, 75d, ARNE VEUM 72, VISIT FLÅM 66a, VISIT FLÅM /PHOTOGRAPHER PER EIDE 21a, 66b, VISIT FLÅM /PHOTOGRAPHER ROLF M. SØRENSEN 2, 8b, 21b, 34, 36, 37, 42b, 43, 44, 45, 56, 67a, 67b, 68, COVER PHOTO Helge Sunde

English translation: Jan Talsethagen
Graphic design: SKALD
Repro Scanner4
Print Valdres Trykkeri as

© SKALD AS 2002
5th edition (2011)
Telephone +47 57 65 41 55
e-mail: forlag@skald.no
www.skald.no

ISBN 978-82-7959-028-6 (Norwegian edition)
ISBN 978-82-7959-029-3 (English edition)
ISBN 978-82-7959-057-6 (German edition)
ISBN 978-82-7959-058-3 (Russian edition)
ISBN 978-82-7959-059-0 (Chinese edition)
ISBN 978-82-7959-061-3 (Japanese edition)
ISBN 978-82-7959-091-0 (Spanish edition)

The Flåm Railway flaamsbana@visitflam.com | www.flaamsbana.no | www.visitflam.no
The Flåm Railway Museum postmaster@flaamsbanen.no | www.flaamsbanen.no